Our Young Voices

Spoken Word Cafe

Patrick Henry School

Cleveland, Ohio

November 10, 2016

Our Young Voices, Spoken Word Cafe Patrick Henry School, © 2016 by Universal Prosperity.

All rights reserved. Printed in the United States of America. No part of this book may be used or reproduced in any manner whatsoever without written permission except in the case of brief quotations embodied in critical articles or reviews.

This book is a work of non-fiction.

For information contact: info@uptownmediaventures.com

Book and Cover design by Team Uptown

ISBN: 978-1-68121-058-2

10 9 8 7 6 5 4 3 2 1

Dedicated to inspiring and enabling youth with the experience of expressing themselves with the written and spoken word!

Patrick Henry School

Table of Contents

Introduction   7

Statements by Supporters of the
    Our Young Voices Initiative   9

Photo Album

The Spoken Word Cafe Poets   23

Kevin Conwell and the Footprints Band   29

Patrick Henry Spoken Word Café Guests   39

Patrick Henry School Staff   47

Page left intentionally blank

Introduction

The *Our Young Voices* publication is one of the manifestations of the *Pride In Authorship Initiative* that seeks to promote expression, written or otherwise, by our youth.

Another part of this initiative is the participation in *Youth Literary and Writing Contests*. The winning essays will be published in the *Our Young Voices* publication, with the winner's photo (if available at printing time), and available on major book retailing web sites like Amazon.com and Barnes & Noble.com.

This publication serves to document the cultural activities and achievements of our young people who participated in the Patrick Henry School's *Spoken Word Café* which was held on November 10, 2016. Any cultural expression by our young people, literary or otherwise, should be celebrated because the youth are our future!

Kevin Conwell

City of Cleveland City Councilman, Ward 9

Kevin Conwell

City of Cleveland Councilman

"It is our civic duty to support worthwhile initiatives to promote scholarship and intellectual development in our community. Infinite Scholars has developed a respected national reputation in providing financial aid to college bound students. Our Young Voices is well on its way to developing a similar track record in encouraging young people in literary and spoken word expression."

Yvonne M. Conwell

Cuyahoga County Councilwoman

District 7

"I am proud to lend support to any initiative that helps to inspire our young people. Programs such as Our Young Voices are great vehicles to inspire our young people to reach for the stars. The, ultimate, end results can only be positive for our community."

Larry Gray

Board Chair Universal Prosperity

"As the Director of Public Information for the Cleveland Fire Department, I have been involved in many public service activities that benefit the public at large. I have always had a keen desire to positively influence our youth – the future of our society.

As fortuity would have it, I was presented with the idea of starting an initiative for the benefit of our youth. The initiative, ultimately, became the *Pride in Authorship Initiative*. The folks at a small publishing house, *Uptown Media Joint Ventures*, committed to insure the publication of this seminal book called *Our Young Voices*.

After much behind the scenes preparation, I am proud to announce the successful publication of another volume of *Our Young Voices*.

This is surely just the beginning and we thank all of our sponsors, supporters, and everyone who has contributed to this extremely worthwhile initiative. So please join us, as we celebrate our young spoken word poets!"

Winston Gragg

President African American Music Association and Member of the Infinite Scholars Board of Directors

"My idea for being involved with *Our Young Voices* is to make a concentrated effort to helping young people by inspiring them. Walt Disney prepares young children to go to Disney, and we want to prepare kids in elementary and middle school to go to college to get an education. Part of this preparation involves giving them opportunities to express themselves, whether by written or spoken word. In order to teach young people, you have to get their attention, and that is exactly what *Our Young Voices* is doing."

Dimitrios Kalafatis

Special Events Coordinator
Golden Corral

"Children are our future and I am, personally, proud to support such worthy causes and programs such as Infinite Scholars and the *Our Young Voices* initiative. Golden Corral is committed to the improvement of society-at-large by supporting such noteworthy civic organizations and programs."

EB Smith

M.P.A., Author, Educator
Media Associate for the
African American Music Association
Vice President, E.B. Smith Project LLC

"Higher education helps develop a person's inner gifts. Student's minds are sharpened with the knowledge and critical thinking skills necessary to compete. I am pleased to be involved with the African American Music Association of Cleveland, Ohio and their continued effort in providing access for young people to get to college. I also support the efforts of *Our Young Voices* in promoting literary expression among our youth. My life serves as proof that their life will be better with it."

Jean Wilson

Executive Administrator
African American Music Association

"*Our Young Voices* gives children and teens an opportunity to express their idea in a public forum. It teaches them how to communicate both written and verbally. Developing these skills at an early age also helps young people to build high self-esteem as well as interpersonal (dealing with others) and intrapersonal communication skills. Students also learn key competencies such as: the ability to solve problems, how to control thoughts and actions, use of critical thinking skills, and the ability to motivate others. We are really excited about the *Our Young Voices* program, because it is making a difference in young people's lives."

Photo Album

The Spoken Word Cafe

Patrick Henry School
Cleveland, Ohio

The Spoken Word Cafe was held Thursday, November 10, 2016 at the Patrick Henry School. The event was supported by City of Cleveland Councilman, Kevin Conwell; Mrs. Yvonne Conwell, Cuyahoga County Council Representative; Universal Prosperity, Uptown Media Joint Ventures, along with many others.

The main attraction was all the young Spoken Word artists who all were eighth grade students. The various renditions were performed in spirited and eloquent fashions.

The students were joined by various staff in poetic expressions, including Ms. B. Anderson, the Aspiring Principal, along with other staff members.

Other highlights included an upbeat musical presentation by Kevin Conwell and the Footprints Band. Also, uplifting statements were made by various Patrick Henry staff including: Principal, Mrs. M. Martin; Aspiring Principal, Ms. B. Anderson; Assistant Principal, Mr. R. Shaw; and Dean of Engagement, Mr. M. Jester.

This publication certainly is another representation of the dedication to inspiring our youth and service in the community.

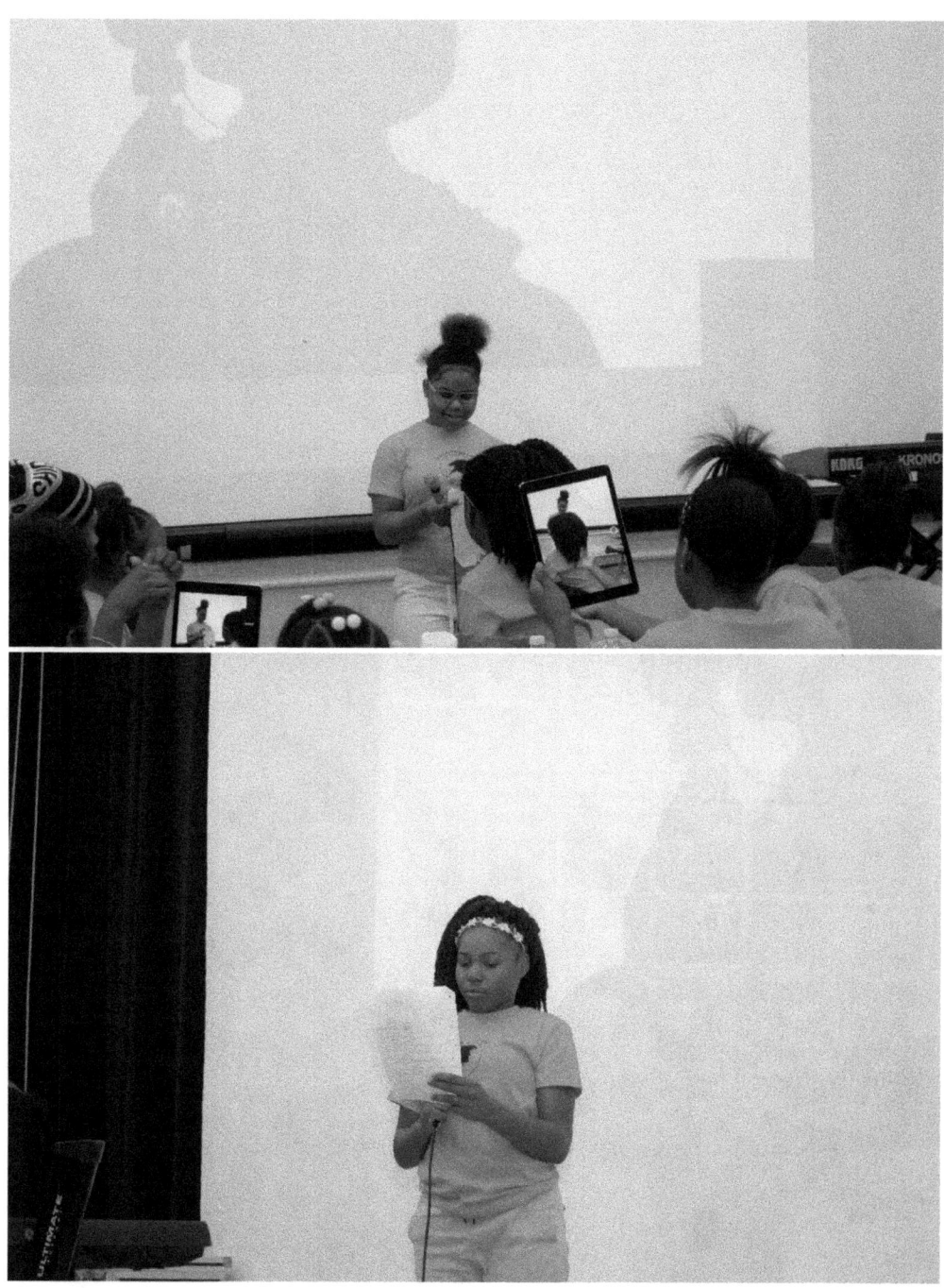

Patrick Henry School

Spoken Word Cafe

Patrick Henry School

Spoken Word Cafe

The Spoken Word Cafe

Kevin Conwell and the Footprints Band

Kevin Conwell and the Footprints certainly delivered musically, giving an enjoyable upbeat performance! The line-up included Kevin Conwell on drums, Ruthie on vocals, JT on sax, along with a host of other musicians on keyboards, bass, and guitar.

The band was also joined by a young drummer - a Patrick Henry Student, who showed off his skills.

Patrick Henry School

Spoken Word Cafe

Patrick Henry School

Spoken Word Cafe

Patrick Henry School

Spoken Word Cafe

37

Patrick Henry School

Spoken Word Cafe

The Spoken Word Cafe

Patrick Henry School
Guests

40

Spoken Word Cafe

Patrick Henry School

Spoken Word Cafe

Patrick Henry School

Spoken Word Cafe

Patrick Henry School

Spoken Word Cafe

The Spoken Word Cafe

Patrick Henry School

Staff

Spoken Word Cafe

Patrick Henry School

Patrick Henry School

A Proud Supporter of:

Our Young Voices is a Pride in Authorship Initiative publication. The young authors selected have successfully conveyed their thoughts, dreams, and concerns by the written word. They deserve to be celebrated!

**2016
Cleveland, Ohio Chapter
Scholarship Week**
Banquet
College Fair
Our Young Voices Dream Contest

Patrick Henry School

Spoken Word Cafe

INFINITE ∞ SCHOLARS

"The Possibilities are Infinite"

During the past decade, the Infinite Scholars Program has served more than 100,000 students and has facilitated more than 1 Billion Dollars in scholarships and financial aid.

Infinite Scholarship Fairs are located in 27 cities and growing. We connect students with scholarship and financial aid opportunities from participating colleges. There is no cost to students or colleges to attend our fairs.

Nearly 300 colleges and universities annually participate in our scholarship fairs. Each fair hosts between 50 and 100 colleges. Our Featured Colleges provide Infinite Scholars with additional support beyond attending our scholarship fairs.

http://www.infinitescholar.org/

Patrick Henry School

Supporters of Our Young Voices Can get their books published and keep 100% control and profits of their book for only $250!

Mention "Our Young Voices" on the "Contact Us" Page or VIA E-Mail

Easy Self-Publishing

http://uptownmediaventures.com

(Click the Publishing Page)

Forward E-Mail Inquiries to:

uptownliterary@gmail.com

Our Young Voices

Spoken Word Cafe
Patrick Henry School

Cleveland, Ohio
November 10, 2016

Patrick Henry School

www.ingramcontent.com/pod-product-compliance
Lightning Source LLC
Chambersburg PA
CBHW081021040426
42444CB00014B/3310